PREDATOR
VS. PREY

BY LEE MARTIN

SCHOLASTIC

Published by Tangerine Press, an imprint of Scholastic Inc.,
557 Broadway, New York, NY 10012
Scholastic Canada Ltd., Markham, Ontario
Grolier International, Inc., Makati City, Philippines

an imprint of
SCHOLASTIC
www.scholastic.com

Produced by becker&mayer!
11120 NE 33rd Place, Suite 101
Bellevue, WA 98004
www.beckermayer.com

becker&mayer!
BOOK PRODUCERS

If you have questions or comments about this book, please visit www.beckermayer.com/customerservice and click on Customer Service Request Form.

Editor: Ben Grossblatt
Designer: Rosanna Brockley
Image Researcher: Katie del Rosario
Production Coordinator: Tom Miller
Managing Editor: Amelia Riedler
Research Assistant: David Lister
Illustrator: Greg Cook

Cover: Lion attacking kudu in Etosha National Park, Namibia
Title page: Cheetah chasing Thomson's gazelle in Masai Mara National Park, Kenya

Image credits: Cover: Lion chasing prey © Martin Harvey/Peter Arnold/Getty Images. Title page: Cheetah © tbkmedia.de/Alamy. Page 4: American alligator with turtle © Martin Woike/Foto Natura/Minden Pictures/Getty Images; American alligator © Michael Patrick O'Neill/Alamy. Page 5: Alligator gar © Reinhard Dirscherl/Alamy; opossum playing dead © Charles Schug/iStockphoto. Page 6: Arctic fox leaping © All Canada Photos/Alamy. Page 7: Willow ptarmigan © Ryerson Clark/iStockphoto; lemming © blickwinkel/Alamy. Page 8: Arctic wolf stalking © Matthew Jacques/Shutterstock; arctic wolf chasing musk oxen © Jim Brandenburg/National Geographic Stock. Page 9: Musk ox © All Canada Photos/Alamy; caribou © Dawn Nichols/iStockphoto. Page 10: Bengal tiger snarling © ZSSD/Minden Pictures; tiger hauling prey © Anup Shah/Nature Picture Library. Page 11: Sambar © Maitree Laipitaksin/Shutterstock; muntjac © D. Trozzo/Alamy. Page 12: Caracal © Anup Shah/Getty Images. Page 13: Gerenuk © Peter Malsbury/iStockphoto; rock hyrax © Emil von Maltitz/Alamy. Page 14: Cheetah pouncing on prey © Charlie Summers/Nature Picture Library. Page 15: Thomson's gazelle © Bruce Block/iStockphoto; desert warthog © Image Focus/Shutterstock. Page 16: Fossa © Mark Carwardine/Getty Images. Page 17: Highland streaked tenrec © Dante Fenolio/Photo Researchers/Getty Images; sifaka © scorpion/iStockphoto. Page 18: Golden eagle with kill © Arco Images GmbH/Alamy; eagle in flight © Dirkr/Dreamstime. Page 19: Hoary marmot pair © DGF72/Shutterstock; snowshoe hare © Photoshot Holdings Ltd/Alamy. Page 20: Golden jackal © blickwinkel/Alamy. Page 21: Kirk's dik-dik © Bill Eagle/Alamy; flamingos in flight © Steffen Foerster Photography/Shutterstock. Page 22: Gray wolf © Image Source/Getty Pictures. Page 23: Moose © Frank Leung/iStockphoto; beaver © Brian Lasenby/Shutterstock. Page 24: Great horned owl and mouse © Michael Durham/Minden Pictures/Getty Images; owl in flight © Scenic Shutterbug/Shutterstock. Page 25: Striped skunk © Arco Images GmbH/Alamy; woodchuck © Studiotouch/Shutterstock. Page 26: Great white shark © Steve Bloom Image/Alamy. Page 27: South American fur seal and loggerhead sea turtle © Michael Patrick O'Neill/Alamy. Page 28: Green anaconda in the water © Alicia Gonzalez/Alamy; anaconda and prey © Francois Gohier/ardea. Page 29: Capybara © Picture Hooked/Malcolm Schuyl/Alamy; collared peccary © Sylvia Schug/iStockphoto. Page 30: Grizzly bear snarling © Scott E. Read/Shutterstock; grizzly with prey © Juniors Bildarchiv/Alamy. Page 31: Rocky mountain bighorn sheep © Bob Reynolds/Shutterstock; mountain goat © Accent Alaska.com/Alamy. Page 32: Jaguar stalking © Rechitan Sorin/Shutterstock; jaguar with armadillo kill © Nick Gordon/Nature Picture Library. Page 33: Two-toed sloth © JJM Stock Photographs/Alamy; tapir © Lajos Endrédi/Dreamstime. Page 34: Komodo dragon © Danita Delimont/Alamy. Page 35: Water buffalo © Uryadnikov Sergey/Shutterstock; deer in the water © Mike Lane/Alamy. Page 36: Leopard with prey © Anup Shah/Nature Picture Library. Page 37: Chacma baboon © SouWest Photography/Shutterstock; giant elands © Danita Delimont/Alamy. Page 38: Leopard seal © Troels Jacobsen/Arcticphoto/Nature Picture Library. Page 39: Emperor penguin © prochasson frederic/Shutterstock; crabeater seal © Dmytro Pylypenko/Shutterstock. Page 40: Lion © Peter Blackwell/Nature Picture Library. Page 41: Zebras running © Mogens Trolle/Shutterstock; giraffe © Theodore Mattas/Shutterstock. Page 42: Nile crocodile and wildebeest © Anup Shah/Nature Picture Library; crocodile snarling © Frans Lanting Studio/Alamy. Page 43: Wildebeest running © Eric Isselée/Shutterstock; hippopotamus © Uryadnikov Sergey/Shutterstock. Page 44: Ocelot © Andy Poole/Shutterstock. Page 45: Southern tamandua © All Canada Photos/Alamy; armadillo © Arto Hakola/Shutterstock. Page 46: Orca © Francois Gohier/ardea. Page 47: Antarctic minke whale © Joanne Weston/Dreamstime; porpoise © Dougall Photography/iStockphoto. Page 48: Peregrine falcon in flight © shootnikonrawstock/Alamy; falcon grabbing prey © Ben Horton/National Geographic Stock. Page 49: Mourning dove © Ashok Rodrigues/iStockphoto; brown bat © Ivan Kuzmin/Shutterstock. Page 50: Polar bear on ice © All Canada Photos/Alamy; polar bear with seal prey © Patricio Robles Gil/Minden Pictures/National Geographic Stock. Page 51: Harp seal © Brian J. Skerry/National Geographic Stock; walrus fight © Prisma Bildagentur AG/Alamy. Page 52: Puma pouncing © Dennis Donohue/Dreamstime; puma with prey © Francois Savigny/Nature Picture Library. Page 53: Elk © Rafael Angel Irusta Machin/Dreamstime; badger © visceralimage/Shutterstock. Page 54: Red fox with pigeon © Laurent Geslin/Nature Picture Library; fox pouncing © David Hosking/Alamy. Page 55: Cottontail rabbit © John James Henderson/Dreamstime; white-footed mouse © Rolf Nussbaumer Photography/Alamy. Page 56: Serval © blickwinkel/Alamy. Page 57: Spoonbill © MartinMaritz/Shutterstock; scrub hare © Peter Betts/Shutterstock. Page 58: Spotted hyena snarling © Andy Diamond/iStockphoto; hyena with prey © Anup Shah/Nature Picture Library. Page 59: Impala © Stefanie van der Vinden/Shutterstock; puff adder © Wildlife GmbH/Alamy. Page 60: Western diamondback rattlesnake © Photoshot Holdings Ltd/Alamy. Page 61: Prairie dog © Mrakoplas/Shutterstock; prairie vole © All Canada Photos/Alamy. Page 62: Wolverine hunting © tbkmedia.de/Alamy; wolverine with prey in the snow © blickwinkel/Alamy. Page 63: Musk deer © Redmond O. Durrell/Alamy; porcupine © Gordon Hunter/iStockphoto. Design elements (throughout): Lightning bolts © TyBy/Shutterstock; cat eyes in dark © Oculo/Shutterstock; medieval weaponry © Goran J/Shutterstock; hourglass © Vector/Shutterstock; ruler symbol © Miguel Angel Salinas Salinas/Shutterstock. Back cover: Snarling puma © Chris Sargent/Dreamstime.

304893 6/12
Printed in Jefferson City, Missouri
10 9 8 7 6 5 4 3 2 1
ISBN: 978-0-545-47962-2
11912
Complies with CPSIA

Predators hunt. Prey animals try to avoid being caught and killed. But there's so much more to the story than that. Both predator and prey are equipped with a stunning variety of tools to stay alive.

AMERICAN ALLIGATOR

Reptiles, mammals, birds, and fish all thrive in the swamps, lakes, and slow-moving rivers of the American Southeast. These wetlands offer a good home to predator and prey, with plenty of water, warm temperatures, and an abundance of plant life.

AMERICAN ALLIGATOR

This menacing giant rules the waterways of the Southeast. The largest reptiles in North America, American alligators use their powerful jaws and a sneak attack to catch their prey. Although they prefer being in the water, gators can move quickly on land. Because their eyes are on top of their heads and their nostrils point upward on their long snouts, they can submerge their bodies entirely. Only their eyes can be seen as they patrol the waters watching for prey. When an unsuspecting animal comes too close—SNAP! The gator lunges and grabs the animal with its huge jaws and drags it into the water to eat it.

SCIENTIFIC NAME: *Alligator mississippiensis*

TYPICAL LENGTH: 12 feet (3.7 m)

PREY: turtles, fish, snakes, and mammals such as deer and opossum

PREDATOR STYLES

 PATIENCE POWER SIZE  STEALTH

Too Big to Chew

Any animal in or near the water is a large alligator's potential dinner. If an alligator bites an animal that is too big to swallow, it drags it into the water and spins with the animal in a death roll, shaking it apart into bite-sized pieces. When an alligator hunts fish or other animals underwater, it closes its nostrils, throat, and ears. That way it can open its jaws and nab its prey without getting water in its lungs.

In the water, most prey animals rely on speed to make a getaway. On land, the profusion of plants and trees provides places to hide. But one small animal has a very special trick to help it avoid being munched.

ALLIGATOR GAR

This huge, prehistoric-looking fish is not related to the alligator, but it does have a large, flattened head that resembles an alligator's. Though rarely preyed upon by large gators, alligator gars occasionally end up on the losing end of a gator attack. Gar have heavily scaled bodies and wide mouths filled with needle-sharp teeth. But the gar's best method to avoid becoming the alligator's lunch is evasion. It uses its speed to thrash away from the giant's jaws as quickly as it can.

SCIENTIFIC NAME: *Atractosteus spatula*

TYPICAL LENGTH: 10 feet (3 m)

SURVIVAL STRATEGIES

SIZE   SPEED

VIRGINIA OPOSSUM

When threatened, the slow, solitary opossum may drool excessively, giving the impression that it's diseased. But the opossum has an even better trick: playing dead. (Many predators don't like to eat prey that is already dead.) When it gets in serious trouble, the opossum goes limp and falls over on its side. Even its breathing is hard to detect. When the danger passes, the opossum gets up and waddles away.

SCIENTIFIC NAME: *Didelphis virginiana*

TYPICAL LENGTH: 2.5 feet (.8 m)

SURVIVAL STRATEGIES

DECEPTION

In the extreme cold of the Arctic winter, animals have adapted different ways of staying warm and hiding from predators and prey. Some grow thick coats, some grow white fur or feathers, and some hide in the safety of burrows.

ARCTIC FOX

Its short muzzle, ears, and legs help the arctic fox conserve heat. Also, the bottoms of its paws are covered with fur, giving it traction on snow and ice. In the winter, it grows a thick white coat of fur, which helps it sneak up on its prey. Arctic foxes rely on their extremely sensitive hearing to find prey. By listening, they can locate prey under the snow. Then, they leap high into the air and pounce, breaking through the snow and trapping the prey beneath.

SCIENTIFIC NAME: *Alopex lagopus*

TYPICAL LENGTH: 3.3 feet (1 m)

PREY: lemmings, birds, and fish

Changing Coats

In summer, the arctic fox's coat changes to brown or gray so that it can blend in among the plants and rocks. Sometimes the fox will follow a polar bear, the Arctic's top predator, so it can eat its leftovers.

PREDATOR STYLES

 CAMOUFLAGE   HEARING   POUNCING   STEALTH

Animals of the Arctic have adapted a variety of ways to hide from predators. Here are two animals with different techniques.

WILLOW PTARMIGAN

The ptarmigan's most interesting adaptation against predators isn't its winter-white or summer-brown coloring. If a predator comes sniffing around, a ptarmigan may simply freeze, but it also may pretend to be injured, dragging one wing on the ground and leading the predator away from the bird's mate or nest. Then, when the predator comes for the "injured" bird, the wily prey manages to fly a short distance and escape.

SCIENTIFIC NAME: *Lagopus lagopus*

TYPICAL LENGTH: 16 inches (40 cm)

SURVIVAL STRATEGIES

 CAMOUFLAGE
 DECEPTION
 FLIGHT
 STILLNESS

NORWAY LEMMING

These little rodents spend the Arctic winter burrowed under the snow hunting for bulbs to eat. Luckily, they have very thick fur that helps insulate them from the cold. Though they are usually solitary animals, they do use threat and alarm calls to warn of danger. Their fur is mottled brown, which helps camouflage them in summer. But in winter they don't have much—other than their burrows—to keep them safe from predators.

SCIENTIFIC NAME: *Lemmus lemmus*

TYPICAL LENGTH: 6 inches (15 cm)

SURVIVAL STRATEGIES

 HIDING SIGNALING

ARCTIC WOLF

The Arctic is a land of ice, snow, and wind. Arctic winters are punishingly cold. It can get as cold as -58°F (-50°C) in the Arctic. The animals that live in the Far North are specially adapted for life in this hostile environment.

ARCTIC WOLF

A beautiful coat of thick white fur distinguishes the arctic wolf from other wolves. It also has smaller ears and padded paws that help keep it warm. Like other wolves, the arctic wolf is a pack animal led by an alpha male and an alpha female. To take down a large animal, such as a musk ox, wolves in the pack work together. They track and surround the herd of musk oxen, frightening and confusing the animals, until they can separate one musk ox from the others. The arctic wolves then charge and go in for the kill. A large prey animal can feed an entire pack for several days.

SCIENTIFIC NAME: *Canis lupus arctos*

TYPICAL LENGTH: 6 feet (1.8 m)

PREY: musk oxen, caribou, ptarmigan, seals, and lemmings

PREDATOR STYLES

CAMOUFLAGE   HEARING   PACK   SMELLING

Good Senses

The arctic wolf's acute senses of hearing and smell help it hunt in an unforgiving environment. Wolves can smell prey animals from incredible distances. Sometimes they have to travel 100 miles (160 km) to find prey. They can go for several days without food and can eat huge amounts at one time.

MUSK OX

This lumbering herd animal—a musk ox can weigh up to 800 pounds (360 kg)—subsists in winter on moss, lichen, and the stems of trees it finds by pawing through the snow with its hooves. Its long, shaggy hair and thick undercoat help protect it from the cold. When threatened, musk oxen form a circle, protecting the young in the middle. The adults face outward, their sharp horns toward the predator. A musk ox will charge when cornered, using its formidable horns as weapons.

SCIENTIFIC NAME: *Ovibos moschatus*

TYPICAL LENGTH: 7 feet (2.1 m)

SURVIVAL STRATEGIES

 NUMBERS POWER SIZE WEAPONRY

CARIBOU

Caribou have an unusual way of warning herd members that they're in danger. They rear up, and special glands in their ankles send out a smell that alerts the other caribou to danger. Both male and female caribou have antlers, which they may use for defense. Also, the herd provides safety in numbers.

SCIENTIFIC NAME: *Rangifer tarandus*

TYPICAL LENGTH: 7.5 feet (2.3 m)

SURVIVAL STRATEGIES

 NUMBERS SIGNALING WEAPONRY

BENGAL TIGER

The many habitats in eastern India and Bangladesh—grasslands, thick forests, and mangrove swamps—provide abundant food for herbivores and, for carnivores, shadowy enclaves from which they can stalk their prey.

BENGAL TIGER

Tigers are supreme stalk-and-ambush hunters. Their dark stripes make them hard to see as they wait in tall grass or shadowy forests. Tigers are patient hunters and will stalk their prey for up to half an hour. When the prey is near, the tiger charges, using its huge front paws and sharp claws to knock the animal down. Then, the Bengal tiger bites the animal's neck, its 3-inch (7-cm) canine teeth sinking in and suffocating the prey or breaking its spine. If there's anything left from its kill, a Bengal tiger will bury it and come back later for snacks.

SCIENTIFIC NAME: *Panthera tigris tigris*

TYPICAL LENGTH: 10 feet (3 m)

PREY: buffalo, deer, and wild pigs

PREDATOR STYLES

 CAMOUFLAGE PATIENCE POWER SIZE STEALTH

Stripes

When we look at tigers in the zoo, they stand out. But within the shadows of a forest or amid waving grass, a tiger's stripes help it hide, breaking up its outline so it's hard to see where the animal begins and ends. The white spots on the backs of tigers' ears may be a way for tiger mothers to keep track of their cubs.

PREY

Bengal tigers are large animals and require a lot of food. Most of their prey animals will raise an alarm and run when in danger. When faced with such a magnificent hunter, this is probably the best strategy for prey animals to take.

SAMBAR

Sambars are some of the largest members of the deer family. The females travel in small herds, but the males mainly live alone. When threatened, a sambar calls out in alarm and keeps calling until the danger has passed. The male may use his impressive antlers to fight off a predator. Sambars are also known to be good swimmers. Sometimes they try to swim away from predators.

SCIENTIFIC NAME: *Rusa unicolor*

TYPICAL LENGTH: 7 feet (2 m)

SURVIVAL STRATEGIES

 SIGNALING SWIMMING WEAPONRY

MUNTJAC

Muntjacs, smaller members of the deer family, are also known as barking deer because when they sense a predator in the area, they will bark like a dog, alerting others to the danger. The males have short antlers and long upper canine teeth, almost like tusks, which they use to bite eggs and the small animals they feed on. (Muntjacs eat plants, too.) They can also deliver powerful blows with their forelegs.

SCIENTIFIC NAME: *Muntiacus muntjak*

TYPICAL LENGTH: 4 feet (1.2 m)

SURVIVAL STRATEGIES

 SIGNALING WEAPONRY

CARACAL

In the dryer regions of Africa and Asia, animals have found ways to survive with little water. Predators often get the liquid they need from their prey. Smaller prey animals conserve energy by spending the day in caves and burrows. They forage for food in the cool of night. Of course, that's when most hunters are out.

CARACAL

Caracals have especially long back legs that make them agile leapers. They also have exceptional hearing and use their ears to pinpoint their prey. In fact, a caracal's ears are controlled by 20 different muscles. Like most cats, caracals stalk their prey. Caracals are great jumpers. They are able to leap 10 feet (3 m) in the air to snatch a low-flying bird. They've even been known to jump on an ostrich's back.

SCIENTIFIC NAME: *Caracal caracal*

TYPICAL LENGTH: 3.5 feet (1 m)

PREY: birds, rodents, and small antelope

PREDATOR STYLES

 AGILITY HEARING POUNCING POWER STEALTH

Black-eared

The word *caracal* comes from a Turkish word meaning "black-eared." Scientists aren't sure what purpose the long tufts of black fur on the caracal's ears serve. Some say the tufts help caracals hear better. Or perhaps caracals use them to keep insects away. Most scientists think they use them somehow to communicate with other caracals.

Prey animals living in the open lands of the near desert rely on excellent hearing and good hiding skills.

GERENUK

These graceful creatures are a type of gazelle. They often eat by standing on their hind legs and using their front legs to reach for leaves on the high branches of trees. Their large ears help them detect danger. When they hear or see a predator, they freeze and wait, watching for further movement. When seriously alarmed, they bleat loudly in warning.

SCIENTIFIC NAME: *Litocranius walleri*

TYPICAL LENGTH: 5 feet (1.5 m)

SURVIVAL STRATEGIES

HEARING   SIGNALING   STILLNESS

ROCK HYRAX

Although shaped like furry footballs, rock hyraxes are distant relatives of elephants. They have similar teeth and toes, and they even grow little tusks. Rock hyraxes live in large groups. When they eat, they form a circle, heads pointing out, watching for predators. Rock hyraxes use a variety of calls to stay in contact with one another. If one hyrax calls out an alarm, the others scramble for cover. The areas where they live, among rocks and cliffs, provide lots of places to hide.

SCIENTIFIC NAME: *Procavia capensis*

TYPICAL LENGTH: 1.5 feet (.5 m)

SURVIVAL STRATEGIES

HIDING   NUMBERS   SIGNALING

CHEETAH

The hot, bright savannas of eastern and southern Africa are home to incredible diversity. Great herds of antelopes and powerful hunting cats are among the animals that live in these open grasslands.

CHEETAH

Cheetahs are built for the chase. From behind a screen of tall grass or atop a tree limb or termite mound, cheetahs watch their prey, waiting for one animal to stray from the others. After stalking it to within about 50 yards (46 m), the cheetah springs into hot pursuit. It can reach speeds of 71 mph (114 kph) and accelerate like a sports car. The cheetah has only about a minute to close in on its prey and knock it to the ground before getting too tired to continue.

SCIENTIFIC NAME: *Acinonyx jubatus*

TYPICAL LENGTH: 7 feet (2 m)

PREY: gazelles, impalas, rabbits, young warthogs, and kudu

PREDATOR STYLES

CAMOUFLAGE

SPEED

The Aftermath

After tripping its prey and taking it down, the cheetah must rest. The chase is tough on the cheetah—it will be out of breath and will have an elevated body temperature. When it's ready, the cheetah eats quickly, to prevent larger, stronger predators from stealing its kill.

PREY

Some prey animals of the savanna rely on the safety of large flocks. Some rely on their own toughness to survive. But they all keep their eyes peeled for silent predators.

THOMSON'S GAZELLE

Thomson's gazelles travel in shifting herds that can number in the hundreds. But if a gazelle becomes a cheetah's target, it puts on a burst of speed and agility, frantically zigzagging to shake its predator. Thomson's gazelles "pronk"—make a series of stiff-legged jumps—to alert others to danger.

SCIENTIFIC NAME: *Eudorcas thomsonii*

TYPICAL LENGTH: 3.5 feet (1 m)

SURVIVAL STRATEGIES

NUMBERS   SIGNALING   SPEED

DESERT WARTHOG

These sturdy herbivores have several tools in their survival kits: extensive burrows provide protection, and tusks can make a cheetah or other hungry cat think twice about attacking. When young warthogs hear the specialized grunts that warn of predators, they freeze in place before making a dash for safety.

SCIENTIFIC NAME: *Phacochoerus aethiopicus*

TYPICAL LENGTH: 4 feet (1.2 m)

SURVIVAL STRATEGIES

HIDING   SIGNALING   STILLNESS   WEAPONRY

FOSSA

The island of Madagascar lies off the east coast of Africa and is home to a great variety of plant and animal life. The plants and animals have evolved in isolation. More than 80 percent of its plant and animal species aren't found anywhere else on Earth.

FOSSA

It looks like a weasel or a cat, but it's actually related to the mongoose and is the top predator on the island of Madagascar. Fossas spend much of their time jumping from branch to branch in the dense canopy of the rain forest, where their long tails help them balance. They feed on almost anything they can get their paws on. Like cats, fossas sneak up on and ambush their prey. Then, they catch it using their powerful legs and claws. Fossas kill their prey with a quick, sharp bite and sometimes work with a partner to catch especially large lemurs.

SCIENTIFIC NAME: *Cryptoprocta ferox*

TYPICAL LENGTH: 6 feet (1.8 m)

PREY: lemurs, wild pigs, mice, and fish

PREDATOR STYLES

AGILITY | CLIMBING | STEALTH | VISION

Elusive Hunter

Fossas move so quickly that scientists have had difficulty studying them. Researchers have discovered that fossas are not related to cats, in spite of the retractable claws that allow them to climb headfirst down tree trunks. When traveling on the forest floor, fossas walk on the soles of their feet, like bears. Fossas can turn their back feet around and grip branches and trunks with their claws.

PREY

For a rodent or rabbit, a large eagle coming down out of the sky, talons first, must be terrifying. Here's how two species preyed on by golden eagles try to survive.

HOARY MARMOT

Marmots are known for their shrill alarm whistles. Once an alarm goes out, every marmot in the colony runs to a safety burrow near the feeding grounds. Marmots know from the tone of the whistle whether the predator comes from the sky or by land, and if it is close or far away.

SCIENTIFIC NAME: *Marmota caligata*

TYPICAL LENGTH: 20 inches (50 cm)

SURVIVAL STRATEGIES

HIDING   NUMBERS   SIGNALING

SNOWSHOE HARE

The snowshoe hare has several features that help it evade predators. Its white wintertime coat helps it blend into a snowy background. Its excellent hearing allows it to locate predators. And its large hind feet have stiff hairs on the paws, which provide the traction that enables the hares to move quickly on top of the snow, zigzagging and leaping away from predators.

SCIENTIFIC NAME: *Lepus americanus*

TYPICAL LENGTH: 1.5 feet (.5 m)

SURVIVAL STRATEGIES

AGILITY   CAMOUFLAGE   HEARING   SPEED   STILLNESS

GOLDEN JACKAL

Golden jackals live throughout a wide area, including North and East Africa, southeast Europe, and southern Asia.

GOLDEN JACKAL

This member of the dog family is sleek and cunning. Its golden fur gives this jackal its name and helps it blend into the tall grasses of the savanna. A jackal will pounce on smaller prey, killing it with a quick bite to the back of the neck. On the hunt for larger prey, jackals work in pairs, and sometimes more. They use yips, growls, and barks to communicate with one another. They circle, charge, and harass their prey until it becomes exhausted and weak. Then, they go in for the kill.

SCIENTIFIC NAME: *Canis aureus*

TYPICAL LENGTH: 3.3 feet (1 m)

PREY: gazelles, birds, snakes, frogs, fish, and insects

PREDATOR STYLES

CAMOUFLAGE   PACK   SIGNALING

Mother, Father, and Babysitter

Jackals mate for life and live in family groups. Often, an adult family member, called a helper, stays with the pups in the den while the parents go off to hunt. The helper cares for the pups and keeps other predators away.

These animals find food and shelter in the scrublands and lakes of Africa.

KIRK'S DIK-DIK

Dik-diks are small antelopes. Their name may come from the whistling sound they make through their noses. The brown coat of a Kirk's dik-dik offers camouflage, and the animal's tiny size allows it to hide behind bushes or tufts of grass. When it must escape, it launches into a quick, agile, zigzag course through the grass.

SCIENTIFIC NAME: *Madoqua kirkii*

TYPICAL LENGTH: 2 feet (.6 m)

SURVIVAL STRATEGIES

AGILITY CAMOUFLAGE HIDING SPEED

LESSER FLAMINGO

These beautiful pink birds live in flocks of up to one million! Traveling in groups helps them fend off danger. If a predator comes near, they make a running start, then take wing in turns. Their color comes from the algae they eat in the volcanic lakes of Africa.

SCIENTIFIC NAME: *Phoeniconaias minor*

TYPICAL WINGSPAN: 3.5 feet (1 m)

SURVIVAL STRATEGIES

FLIGHT NUMBERS

Wolves once ranged throughout North America, but they now live mostly in Canada, Alaska, and some northern states of the lower 48 United States.

GRAY WOLF

Wolves are social animals. They howl to assemble the pack for a hunt. They use a complex system of vocal signals and body language to communicate as they hunt. They have a very good sense of smell, which helps them locate prey. Hunting in packs of up to 10 animals, wolves can cover as much as 50 miles (80 km) in a day. They take down large prey by leaping on the prey's back and shoulders. A wolf will hunt smaller animals, such as beaver and rabbits, on its own.

SCIENTIFIC NAME: *Canis lupus*

TYPICAL LENGTH: 6 feet (1.8 m)

PREY: elk, deer, moose, beaver, and rabbits

PREDATOR STYLES

 PACK SIGNALING  SMELLING SPEED

Family Unit

A wolf pack is made up of an alpha male and an alpha female, their offspring, and other young wolves. The alpha pair leads the pack and leads the hunt. Wolves in a pack form very close bonds.

Gray wolves, in a pack or alone, are efficient hunters. Animals living in wolf territory must be able to fight or flee.

MOOSE

Moose are the largest members of the deer family, weighing in at up to 1,600 pounds (725 kg). Males grow huge sets of antlers that can be 6 feet (1.8 m) across. Their wide, sharp hooves help support them on snow and in mud. They use both their hooves and their antlers to fight off predators. Moose like water and are good swimmers. On land, they are surprisingly quick, able to run at speeds of up to 35 mph (56 kph) for short distances.

SCIENTIFIC NAME: *Alces americanus*

TYPICAL LENGTH: 9 feet (2.7 m)

SURVIVAL STRATEGIES

 SIZE SPEED SWIMMING  WEAPONRY

BEAVER

Beavers are not quick on land, but in the water they are fast and agile swimmers. They can remain underwater as long as 15 minutes, perhaps long enough for a predator to lose interest. They tend to build their dens in the middle of ponds, accessible by underwater entrances. Beavers slap their large, flat tails on the water to warn other beavers of danger.

SCIENTIFIC NAME: *Castor canadensis*

TYPICAL LENGTH: 3.5 feet (1 m)

SURVIVAL STRATEGIES

 HIDING SIGNALING SWIMMING

GREAT HORNED OWL

These animals hunt and live throughout North and South America—in forests, open woodlands, pastures, farmlands, and maybe even in your neighborhood!

GREAT HORNED OWL

The fiercest hunter of all the owls, great horned owls are powerful enough to take prey two to three times heavier than themselves. From a high perch, they watch for prey with their large yellow eyes. Because of the fringed edges of their wing feathers, they can swoop down silently and snatch an animal with their large talons. Most prey are killed instantly. Great horned owls also hunt by walking on the ground to stalk prey or by wading into shallow water to catch frogs and fish. They swallow most prey whole, regurgitating the undigestible bones, fur, and feathers.

SCIENTIFIC NAME: *Bubo virginianus*

TYPICAL WINGSPAN: 5 feet (1.5 m)

PREY: raccoons, rabbits, squirrels, skunks, mice, rats, and birds

PREDATOR STYLES

FLIGHT   PATIENCE   STEALTH   VISION

Are Those Ears?

The feather tufts, or "horns," on top of the owl's head look like a cat's ears, but they have nothing to do with hearing. Owls use the tufts to communicate with other owls, raising or lowering them depending on their moods.

PREY

The creatures that live in and around the woods in owl territory must always be wary of the silent hunter from above.

STRIPED SKUNK

A skunk's extremely stinky spray is a tried-and-true predator repellent. The skunk's oily liquid spray is produced by glands under its tail. When threatened, the skunk turns its back to its foe and blasts away. The mist can travel as far as 10 feet (3 m) and can burn the eyes of any creature in its path. Most predators steer clear of skunks, but great horned owls and other raptors are undeterred by the stink.

SCIENTIFIC NAME: *Mephitis mephitis*

TYPICAL LENGTH: 2.5 feet (.8 m)

SURVIVAL STRATEGIES

STINK

WOODCHUCK

Also known as groundhogs, woodchucks live alone. They are cautious when they're outside their dens, looking up often while eating to listen and watch for predators. If they detect danger in the area, they'll whistle sharply and then run and hide. Woodchucks have strong, sharp teeth—and will use them to fight for their lives.

SCIENTIFIC NAME: *Marmota monax*

TYPICAL LENGTH: 2 feet (.6 m)

SURVIVAL STRATEGIES

HEARING HIDING SIGNALING WEAPONRY

GREAT WHITE SHARK

Great white sharks have a very wide range. They live in all the world's oceans—cold, temperate, and tropical—and hunt along the coasts. They also travel across the seas to new feeding grounds.

Shark Teeth

Great white sharks have as many as 150 teeth arranged in two or three rows. If a shark loses a tooth, another one swivels up from the backup teeth and takes the lost tooth's place. Sharks grow and use thousands of teeth in a lifetime.

GREAT WHITE SHARK

Great white sharks inspire equal parts fear and admiration. They are fast, efficient killers. Their huge, gaping jaws hold several rows of serrated teeth that cut away mouthfuls of flesh. They are equipped with special organs that pick up electromagnetic fields generated by prey animals, and they can smell tiny amounts of blood in the water up to 3 miles (4.8 km) away. When great whites locate prey, they may zoom up under it, ram it, bite a large chunk out of it—and then circle back to finish their meal.

SCIENTIFIC NAME: *Carcharodon carcharias*

TYPICAL LENGTH: 20 feet (6 m)

PREY: seals, sea lions, dolphins, and sea turtles

PREDATOR STYLES

 POWER
 SIZE
 SMELLING
 WEAPONRY

PREY

The open ocean does not provide many places for prey animals to hide, so they must rely on quickness and other defenses for protection.

SOUTH AMERICAN FUR SEAL

When the seals are on land, they have nothing to fear from sharks. But when they are in the open water feeding on the fish that make up most of their diet, they must rely on speed and agility to escape a predator. A fur seal will make quick turns and may attempt to jump out of the water.

SCIENTIFIC NAME: *Arctocephalus australis*

TYPICAL LENGTH: 5.5 feet (1.7 m)

SURVIVAL STRATEGIES

 AGILITY   SPEED

LOGGERHEAD SEA TURTLE

These sea turtles have huge heads and large jaws. Unlike other species of turtles, sea turtles cannot pull their heads and legs into their shells. But their size, hard shells, and thick, scaly skin help protect them from most predators. If attacked, sea turtles don't hesitate to bite back.

SCIENTIFIC NAME: *Caretta caretta*

TYPICAL LENGTH: 3 feet (.9 m)

SURVIVAL STRATEGIES

 SIZE   TOUGH EXTERIOR

GREEN ANACONDA

The largest rain forests in the world provide a rich habitat for animals and plants. Tens of thousands of unique plant and animal species live in the tropical rain forests that surround the Amazon and Orinoco rivers. One of them is the longest snake in the world.

GREEN ANACONDA

Because of its bulk, the anaconda moves slowly and awkwardly on land. But in the water, it swims with sinuous stealth. The anaconda hunts in the swamps and slow-moving streams of the tropical rain forest, using surprise tactics and strength to catch its prey. It submerges itself in the water—only its eyes and nostrils appear above the surface—and waits for an animal to approach the riverbank. Then, it throws itself at the prey, coiling its body around it and squeezing. When the animal stops breathing, the anaconda opens its jaws and swallows the prey whole, no matter the size.

SCIENTIFIC NAME: *Eunectes murinus*

TYPICAL LENGTH: 30 feet (9 m)

PREY: wild pigs, deer, birds, turtles, capybaras, and caimans

PREDATOR STYLES

Bulky Constrictor

There are longer snakes in the world, but none has as great a girth as the green anaconda. Anacondas are constrictors. Unlike snakes that use venom to kill prey, constrictors coil their bodies around the prey and squeeze until the animal suffocates or is crushed to death. Anacondas use their teeth only to hold on to prey as they constrict it.

With so many animals inhabiting the same area, life in the rain forest can be competitive. Some rain forest animals live in large groups and look out for one another, while others hide or use other defensive tricks.

CAPYBARA

The world's largest rodents, capybaras live near water in groups of 10 to 30. They're good swimmers and use their speed to escape predators. But the main protection capybaras rely on is safety in numbers. They communicate well and use a variety of purrs, barks, and whistles to alert one another to threats. Sometimes a whole group of capybaras will bark to try to scare the predator away.

SCIENTIFIC NAME: *Hydrochoerus hydrochaeris*

TYPICAL LENGTH: 4 feet (1.2 m)

SURVIVAL STRATEGIES

 NUMBERS
 SIGNALING
 SPEED
 SWIMMING

COLLARED PECCARY

These piglike animals live in bands of up to 50, foraging, eating, and sleeping together. The band provides some protection, and with their good sense of hearing, peccaries scatter at the slightest sound of danger. But the peccary also has short, sharp tusks, which are capable of wounding anacondas. Peccaries are sometimes called javelinas.

SCIENTIFIC NAME: *Pecari tajacu*

TYPICAL LENGTH: 3.5 feet (1 m)

SURVIVAL STRATEGIES

 HEARING
 NUMBERS
 WEAPONRY

GRIZZLY BEAR

Their range once covered almost all of North America, but now, greatly reduced in number, grizzly bears live mainly in Alaska and the Canadian Rocky Mountains. The animals of this region thrive in these wild areas where few humans live.

GRIZZLY BEAR

Almost everything about these bears is big. They have massive heads, large noses, long, curved claws, big teeth, and a hump of muscle on their shoulders. Grizzlies have good senses of hearing and smell, which help them locate food sources. For such hefty animals, they can move quickly— up to 35 mph (56 kph) for short distances—and run down their prey. Then, they use their strong front legs to bring the animal down with one blow.

SCIENTIFIC NAME: *Ursus arctos horribilis*

TYPICAL LENGTH: 8 feet (2.5 m)

PREY: moose, deer, bighorn sheep, elk, caribou, mountain goats, and salmon

PREDATOR STYLES

CLIMBING · HEARING · POWER

SIZE · SMELLING · SPEED

Big Appetite

Because they are such enormous animals, grizzlies need to eat a lot during the spring, summer, and fall before they go into hibernation for the winter. Grizzlies are omnivores, which means they eat pretty much anything: roots, berries, insects, lots of salmon, large mammals, and sometimes the leftovers from another animal's kill.

These large hoofed mammals make their home on the steep, precarious cliffs of the Rocky Mountains.

ROCKY MOUNTAIN BIGHORN SHEEP

The most obvious defense these sheep have are their impressive pairs of curved horns. The bottoms of the bighorn sheeps' hooves are rough, and the hooves are split, which gives them a good grip on the rocky cliffs where they live. Their exceptional eyesight helps them navigate the cliffs so they can quickly bound from ledge to ledge, often escaping to safety.

SCIENTIFIC NAME: *Ovis canadensis*

TYPICAL LENGTH: 5.5 feet (1.7 m)

SURVIVAL STRATEGIES

AGILITY CLIMBING SPEED

VISION WEAPONRY

MOUNTAIN GOAT

Each toe of a mountain goat's cloven hoof has a rubbery pad on the bottom that helps the goat scale the rocks. The goats are agile climbers and can leap 10 feet (3 m) as they zigzag up a mountain. In winter, their white coats provide camouflage against the snow. Mountain goats use their horns for defense against predators.

SCIENTIFIC NAME: *Oreamnos americanus*

TYPICAL LENGTH: 5 feet (1.5 m)

SURVIVAL STRATEGIES

AGILITY CAMOUFLAGE CLIMBING WEAPONRY

JAGUAR

These animals live in the rainy, humid rain forests of Central and South America. The trees provide cover for hunting and foraging, and the ponds and rivers provide places for a quick, cooling dip.

Panthers

Panther is a general term that has been used to describe various big cats, such as jaguars, leopards, and pumas. Leopards live only in Africa and Asia, and jaguars live in Central and South America. The two cats' spot patterns are different, and jaguars are stockier, with shorter, thicker tails.

JAGUAR

The largest of South America's big cats, jaguars prowl the forests. They are good swimmers and often kill turtles and caimans, using powerful jaws to sink their teeth into the turtle's shell or the caiman's skull. In fact, piercing the prey's skull is a jaguar's typical method of killing. Their eyes are adapted for hunting at night. They climb trees and lie in wait to ambush their prey, killing it with a pounce and a big bite. In darker parts of the rain forest, the jaguar's coat tends to be darker, helping it hide beneath the shadowy canopy.

SCIENTIFIC NAME: *Panthera onca*

TYPICAL LENGTH: 8 feet (2.4 m)

PREY: armadillos, turtles, tortoises, caimans, peccaries, deer, sloths, and tapirs

PREDATOR STYLES

CAMOUFLAGE CLIMBING POUNCING POWER

STEALTH SWIMMING VISION

The rain forest is home to one of the slowest-moving animals in the world—and one of the strangest-looking.

HOFFMANN'S TWO-TOED SLOTH

Sloths spend most of their time hanging upside down in trees. They move very slowly and sometimes appear green because of the algae growing on them. This helps them hide in the trees. Surprisingly, they are good swimmers and can drop into a river to swim away from a threat. Their long claws help them hang on to tree branches and fight off predators.

SCIENTIFIC NAME: *Choloepus hoffmanni*

TYPICAL LENGTH: 2 feet (.6 m)

SURVIVAL STRATEGIES

 CAMOUFLAGE CLIMBING SWIMMING WEAPONRY

BRAZILIAN TAPIR

The tapir's trunk is actually its nose and upper lip, which it can use to grasp things, much like an elephant does. When in danger, a tapir will try to run away. But if a predator corners it, a tapir will charge. Tapirs can weigh up to 550 pounds (250 kg). That's a lot of weight rumbling across the forest floor!

SCIENTIFIC NAME: *Tapirus terrestris*

TYPICAL LENGTH: 7 feet (2.1 m)

SURVIVAL STRATEGIES

 SIZE SWIMMING

KOMODO DRAGON

The fierce Komodo dragon is found only on a few islands in Indonesia. Life on these islands is harsh—the weather is hot and dry, and there is very little fresh water.

KOMODO DRAGON

The biggest lizard in the world is a meat-eating machine. Komodos use their long forked tongues to sense food up to a mile (1.6 km) away. Then, they hide along a trail, camouflaged by their grayish brown skin, and wait. When an animal walks by, the dragon attacks with its long claws and serrated teeth, pumping venom—among the most powerful in the world of reptiles—into its prey. The prey might get away, but the dragon slowly follows along, scenting the animal with its tongue. Eventually, the animal will die from blood loss or from the venom (and not from deadly bacteria found in the dragon's bite, as previously thought).

SCIENTIFIC NAME: *Varanus komodoensis*

TYPICAL LENGTH: 9 feet (2.7 m)

PREY: wild pigs, deer, water buffalo, and snakes

PREDATOR STYLES

  CAMOUFLAGE PATIENCE POWER SIZE  SMELLING SWIMMING VENOM

Deadly Dragon

Komodo dragons can weigh up to 300 pounds (140 kg). And though lumbering, they're strong and surprisingly athletic. They can run for short distances and they're good swimmers. Komodo dragons have about 60 teeth and can go through five sets of teeth in a lifetime. Their skulls are flexible, which allows them to swallow huge hunks of food. A Komodo dragon can eat up to 80 percent of its body weight in one meal.

PREY

Small Indonesian islands are full of dangers. The hot, dry weather is bad enough. But the presence of the dragons makes things even tougher. A Komodo's prey has to be just as tough.

WATER BUFFALO

The water buffalo's massive horns, which can be 5 feet (1.5 m) across, make most predators reconsider attacking. When threatened, water buffalo will stand together and charge as a group. But if a Komodo dragon even nips it on the leg, the buffalo will be dead within days.

SCIENTIFIC NAME: *Bubalus bubalis*

TYPICAL LENGTH: 8 feet (2.4 m)

SURVIVAL STRATEGIES

 NUMBERS POWER SIZE WEAPONRY

TIMOR DEER

These small deer sport impressive sets of antlers. In the spring, the male deer decorate their antlers with grasses and moss to attract females and deter competitors. The deer congregate in herds, and their dusty brown coats help them hide. When frightened, a stag lets out a loud bark, alerting other deer to danger.

SCIENTIFIC NAME: *Rusa timorensis*

TYPICAL LENGTH: 5 feet (1.5 m)

SURVIVAL STRATEGIES

 CAMOUFLAGE NUMBERS SIGNALING WEAPONRY

LEOPARD

These creatures are highly adaptable. They are able to live in a variety of habitats, from Africa to Asia. Leopards prefer to hunt under the cover of tall grasses or trees.

LEOPARD

Leopards are classic feline hunters. They stalk their prey from behind tall grasses, or they hide in trees. Its spots blending in with the leaves, a leopard pounces on its prey. Leopards are all-around good athletes. They're strong swimmers and can sprint at speeds of up to 36 mph (58 kph). They can leap more than 20 feet (6 m) and jump 10 feet (3 m) straight up. They hunt at night, using their keen senses of vision and hearing to find their prey. They kill with a bite to the neck.

SCIENTIFIC NAME: *Panthera pardus*

TYPICAL LENGTH: 9 feet (2.7 m)

PREY: monkeys, baboons, fish, and antelope

PREDATOR STYLES

CAMOUFLAGE CLIMBING HEARING POUNCING

POWER SPEED SWIMMING VISION

Strong and Agile

Leopards are super-strong. They often drag a heavy kill up into a tree to protect it from scavengers. Leopards spend quite a bit of time in trees, and they often rest on branches during the heat of the day.

Trees provide food and places to hide. But they also conceal dangers. How do prey animals protect themselves?

CHACMA BABOON

These baboons live on the ground, and they venture into trees to escape predators, eat, or sleep. Baboons live in groups called troops. All members help forage for food and raise the young. To defend themselves, baboons have large, sharp teeth and can run fast. Male chacma baboons make a "wahoo" call when big cats are around. Big male baboons will gang up on a large predator such as a leopard, sometimes injuring it as they try to chase it away.

SCIENTIFIC NAME: *Papio ursinus*

TYPICAL LENGTH: 5 feet (1.5 m)

SURVIVAL STRATEGIES

CLIMBING   NUMBERS   SIGNALING

SPEED   WEAPONRY

GIANT ELAND

Giant elands are the largest of the antelopes. Even though they're big, they are quick and nimble. They live in herds of 20 or more, and they have impressive, corkscrewed horns. They use their horns to break off branches to eat. But at up to 4 feet (1.2 m) long, these horns can be used for defense as well.

SCIENTIFIC NAME: *Taurotragus derbianus gigas*

TYPICAL LENGTH: 9.5 feet (2.9 m)

SURVIVAL STRATEGIES

AGILITY   NUMBERS   SPEED   WEAPONRY

LEOPARD SEAL

All the animals that live in and around the frigid waters of the Antarctic Ocean have adapted to survive in this unforgiving environment.

LEOPARD SEAL

Like leopards, leopard seals are spotted and fierce. Their large heads and gaping jaws are designed to help them kill and eat prey. They are the only seals that prey on warm-blooded animals such as other seals. Leopard seals are fast, agile swimmers, always on the prowl for prey. Sometimes they wait just under an ice shelf to snatch penguins that slip into the water, shaking them until they've skinned them.

SCIENTIFIC NAME: *Hydrurga leptonyx*

TYPICAL LENGTH: 10 feet (3 m)

PREY: penguins, fish, and seals

PREDATOR STYLES

 AGILITY PATIENCE POWER SPEED SWIMMING

Nonstop Hunting

Leopard seals have been known to attack humans, perhaps from hunger or maybe just out of curiosity. While one of explorer Ernest Shackleton's crew members was skiing across the ice, a leopard seal lunged at him. The man skied away as quickly as he could, but the seal dived into the water and stayed with him, following his shadow.

PREY

Seals spend only about 10 percent of their time out of the water, so penguins are more or less safe when they are on the pack ice. For most animals that live in the Antarctic, a thick layer of blubber helps insulate their bodies from the cold.

EMPEROR PENGUIN

These are the largest of all penguins. They get through the long Antarctic winters by huddling together in a huge mass, adults and young together. Young penguins are preyed upon in the summer when they leave the group to fish. Emperor penguins are fast in the water and may use voice calls to warn one another of predators.

SCIENTIFIC NAME: *Aptenodytes forsteri*

TYPICAL LENGTH: 3.5 feet (1 m)

SURVIVAL STRATEGIES

NUMBERS · SIGNALING · SPEED

CRABEATER SEAL

Actually, these seals don't eat crabs at all but instead consume tiny shrimplike crustaceans called krill. In fact, they eat tons of krill each year! They have special teeth that form a strainer, which keeps the krill in their mouths while they force the water out. They are big and fast swimmers. Most leopard seals prey on younger crabeaters, catching them while swimming.

SCIENTIFIC NAME: *Lobodon carcinophaga*

TYPICAL LENGTH: 7.5 feet (2.3 m)

SURVIVAL STRATEGIES

AGILITY · SPEED · SWIMMING

LION

Long known as "the king of beasts," the lion rules the great savannas, the open grassy plains of Africa. Many animals make this area their home, including massive herds of migrating zebras, wildebeests, and gazelles.

Defender of the Pride

The pride is led by the dominant female, but the male acts as the defender. He keeps predators away from the cubs and guards his mates. But he can be overthrown if a younger lion challenges him to a fight and wins.

LION

It is the females, not the males, that do most of the hunting for the pride. Lions are the only wild cats that live in groups of related females. The females hunt in groups or pairs, stalking their prey. When they get close to their target, they lunge and bite the animal's neck, suffocating it. The lion's back teeth are designed to work like scissors, helping them slice through meat.

SCIENTIFIC NAME: *Panthera leo*

TYPICAL LENGTH: 10 feet (3 m)

PREY: antelopes, zebras, wildebeests, warthogs, and giraffes

PREDATOR STYLES

CAMOUFLAGE   PACK   POWER   STEALTH

The savannas provide space for large herds, plenty of grass and tree leaves, and, in the wet season, water. But these herd animals must constantly be on the lookout for danger.

PLAINS ZEBRA

Scientists aren't exactly sure about the function of a zebra's stripes, but they may serve to confuse predators. One zebra among many can be difficult to distinguish, especially at night. Zebras live in family groups within a larger herd. If one of their members is hurt, they will circle the injured animal and work to drive off predators with powerful kicks of their hind legs.

SCIENTIFIC NAME: *Equus quagga burchelli*

TYPICAL LENGTH: 7.5 feet (2.3 m)

SURVIVAL STRATEGIES

CAMOUFLAGE · NUMBERS · POWER

GIRAFFE

Being the world's tallest animals helps giraffes keep an eye out for predators. These long-legged animals are fast runners and can reach speeds of more than 30 mph (48 kph) over short distances. Their spotted coats help them hide in the dappled shade of a tree. If a predator gets too close, it may get pounded by a powerful kick.

SCIENTIFIC NAME: *Giraffa camelopardalis*

TYPICAL HEIGHT: 17 feet (5.2 m)

SURVIVAL STRATEGIES

CAMOUFLAGE · POWER · SIZE · SPEED · WEAPONRY

NILE CROCODILE

Most animals need water. Some live in it. Some drink it. The rivers of northern and southern Africa give life but can also take it away.

NILE CROCODILE

Woe to any creature that comes to the water's edge where crocodiles hide! Crocodiles eat pretty much anything that moves. First, they conceal themselves underwater and wait. When prey comes near, they lunge at the animal, launching themselves onto land, snapping their ferocious jaws around the prey. Then, they drag the prey into the water and roll it around, which drowns it, and tear off chunks of meat. Crocodiles are social animals. They sometimes work together to trap and eat prey.

SCIENTIFIC NAME: *Crocodylus niloticus*

TYPICAL LENGTH: 16 feet (4.9 m)

PREY: wildebeests, zebras, small hippos, and fish

PREDATOR STYLES

 PATIENCE POWER SIZE STEALTH SWIMMING WEAPONRY

Heavy Belly

Crocodiles regularly swallow rocks. Scientists aren't sure why. It may make them heavier, to help them lie on the river bottom when hiding. Or it may help give them mass when they try to overpower prey. Or the rocks they've swallowed may help stabilize them as they swim.

When warding off predators, strength is certainly an advantage. Of course, size and heft help, too.

WILDEBEEST

The name *wildebeest* means "wild beast." And these prehistoric-looking antelopes, also called gnus, do look kind of wild and crazy. They are large and strong, with big heads. And they've got imposing sets of curved horns. Wildebeests gather in huge groups when they migrate.

SCIENTIFIC NAME: *Connochaetes taurinus*

TYPICAL LENGTH: 7 feet (2.1 m)

SURVIVAL STRATEGIES

HIPPOPOTAMUS

As the third-largest animals on land, full-grown hippos don't have much to fear from predators. But smaller, younger hippos are more vulnerable. Their muddy-colored skin helps them hide in muddy rivers. Adults also have tusklike canine teeth that can deliver fearsome bites.

SCIENTIFIC NAME: *Hippopotamus amphibius*

TYPICAL LENGTH: 12 feet (3.7 m)

SURVIVAL STRATEGIES

OCELOT

These animals live in both dense forests and dry scrublands, from Texas to Venezuela. Some require trees to climb. Others require places to hide.

OCELOT

This beautiful small cat patrols the ground at night. Its eyes collect light efficiently. It also uses long whiskers to help it feel its way around. Ocelots thrive in areas where they can hide. They can easily stalk and ambush their prey from these hiding spots. And they can clean a bone with their rough tongues. Though they usually hunt on the ground, ocelots will stalk monkeys and birds in trees. They are also good swimmers.

SCIENTIFIC NAME: *Leopardus pardalis*

TYPICAL LENGTH: 4 feet (1.2 m)

PREY: rabbits, rodents, fish, iguanas, monkeys, and birds

PREDATOR STYLES

AGILITY · CAMOUFLAGE · CLIMBING · POUNCING

STEALTH · SWIMMING · VISION

Picky Eater

An ocelot's teeth aren't designed for chewing food but for tearing off chunks of meat. That doesn't mean the ocelot just gobbles its meals. Ocelots pluck the feathers from birds and remove the fur from mammals before digging in.

The nights are cool and bring predators and prey out of hiding to hunt and forage for food. These two animals have developed creative ways to protect themselves.

SOUTHERN TAMANDUA

The tamandua is a type of anteater that forages for food at night. It has a couple of effective defenses. One is a stinky smell it emits when agitated. Another is a strong set of front legs that end in long, curved claws.

SCIENTIFIC NAME: *Tamandua tetradactyla*

TYPICAL LENGTH: 4 feet (1.2 m)

SURVIVAL STRATEGIES

 STINK WEAPONRY

NINE-BANDED ARMADILLO

Armadillos come equipped with their own armor: a covering of bony scales on their backs. To protect themselves, they hunker down close to the ground, shielding their softer underbellies. If frightened, armadillos may jump 3 feet (.9 m) straight up and then run toward the safety of a burrow.

SCIENTIFIC NAME: *Dasypus novemcinctus*

TYPICAL LENGTH: 2.5 feet (.8 m)

SURVIVAL STRATEGIES

 HIDING TOUGH EXTERIOR

Orcas roam all the world's oceans, though they prefer coastal and colder waters near the poles. The waters there are rich with fish and other sea life—in other words, orca food.

ORCA

Orcas, also called killer whales, are some of the biggest, strongest predators in the sea. They live in groups, called pods. Although orcas will hunt alone, pods often hunt both large and small prey. As they hunt, orcas communicate using a variety of sounds—squeaks, whistles, and clicks. This helps them keep track of one another and their prey. Similar to a pack of wolves, the pod surrounds large prey. Individual whales take turns striking until the prey dies. Orcas' 3-inch (7.6-cm) teeth are built for tearing, not chewing. An orca can swallow bites of meat as large as a seal.

SCIENTIFIC NAME: *Orcinus orca*

TYPICAL LENGTH: 30 feet (9.1 m)

PREY: fish, seals, whales, and squid

PREDATOR STYLES

PACK   POWER   SIGNALING   SIZE

The Pod

The size of a pod can vary from about 10 to more than 50 orcas. Within a pod, members of close family groups swim together. In most pods, young orcas and females swim in the center—and the males remain at the edges. Each pod has its own distinct dialect that it uses to communicate.

There's really no place to hide in the ocean. Most creatures just try to stay well fed—and to avoid becoming another creature's meal!

ANTARCTIC MINKE WHALE

Minke whales are among the smallest of the baleen whales. Baleen whales have rows of plates instead of teeth for sifting tiny shrimp, or krill, from the water. Even so, they are big— roughly the same size as orcas. They are fast swimmers and can reach speeds up to 21 mph (34 kph).

SCIENTIFIC NAME: *Balaenoptera bonaerensis*

TYPICAL LENGTH: 30 feet (9.1 m)

SURVIVAL STRATEGIES

 SIZE SPEED

DALL'S PORPOISE

These porpoises sometimes swim alongside orcas, eating salmon. At other times, they are the orca's dinner! Dall's porpoises can swim at speeds up to 35 mph (56 kph) and are much more agile than orcas. But orcas get around this by taking turns chasing the porpoise.

SCIENTIFIC NAME: *Phocoenoides dalli*

TYPICAL LENGTH: 6 feet (1.8 m)

SURVIVAL STRATEGIES

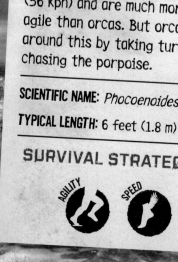 AGILITY  SPEED

PEREGRINE FALCON

Peregrine falcons can be found throughout the world. They prefer to hunt in open or lightly forested areas.

PEREGRINE FALCON

These stealthy masked predators are masters of the sneak attack. Peregrine falcons hunt other birds and bats, striking from above and coming out of nowhere. Their pointed wings power them through the air, and their long tails help them navigate at high speeds. With their keen vision, peregrines locate their prey, fold their wings, and dive steeply, reaching speeds up to 200 mph (320 kph)! They pull their talons into a fist shape and strike prey in midair. If the prey hasn't died from the blow, they use their "killing tooth," a notch in their hooked beak, to break the animal's spinal cord.

SCIENTIFIC NAME: *Falco peregrinus*

TYPICAL WINGSPAN: 3 feet (.9 m)

PREY: songbirds, ducks, and bats

PREDATOR STYLES

AGILITY FLIGHT SPEED STEALTH VISION

City Dwellers

Peregrines have adapted to life in the city. They nest on bridges and on the ledges of tall buildings, which simulate the cliffs where they live in the wild. The pigeons, starlings, and other birds that typically inhabit cities provide them with good hunting and plenty of food.

Peregrine falcons are stealthy and fast hunters. It is a challenge for birds and bats to avoid becoming prey. But almost every animal has some form of defense.

MOURNING DOVE

Mourning doves, named that because of their sad-sounding calls, are capable of flying with great agility as fast as 55 mph (88 kph). This is swift enough to escape from some predators, but not peregrines and other falcons. To distract predators from attacking its nest, a mourning dove pretends to have a broken wing.

SCIENTIFIC NAME: *Zenaida macroura*

TYPICAL WINGSPAN: 1.5 feet (.5 m)

SURVIVAL STRATEGIES

 AGILITY DECEPTION

BIG BROWN BAT

These glossy, copper-colored bats are bigger than other American bats. Their hidden roosts help protect them from predators. They are fast flyers, able to reach speeds up to 40 mph (64 kph). Raptors catch most bats as they leave their roosts to feed.

SCIENTIFIC NAME: *Eptesicus fuscus*

TYPICAL WINGSPAN: 1.2 feet (.4 m)

SURVIVAL STRATEGIES

 HIDING SPEED

POLAR BEAR

The Arctic is brutal. Predator and prey alike face some of the harshest conditions on the planet. Biting cold and winter days when the sun never rises make simple survival tough.

POLAR BEAR

With their size, strength, and smarts, polar bears are the undisputed champions of the Arctic. The largest carnivores on land, polar bears are well suited to the freezing white world in which they hunt and live. The polar bear's predatory style is part power, part patience. When it comes to hunting their favorite prey—seals—they take a wait-and-see approach. They stand motionless on the ice by a seal's breathing hole and wait for their prey. When a seal surfaces and exhales—*WHAM!* The bear hauls the prey onto the ice with one swipe of its mighty paw.

SCIENTIFIC NAME: *Ursus maritimus*

TYPICAL LENGTH: 8 feet (2.4 m)

PREY: Seals, walruses, beluga whales, musk oxen, and reindeer

PREDATOR STYLES

PATIENCE POWER SIZE SWIMMING

Where Ice Meets Water

Like all predators, polar bears live where there is prey. That means they can be found where ice meets water—and not closer to the North Pole, where seals are rare. Depending on where in the Arctic they live, polar bears might touch solid ground only in warmer months, when the ice breaks up. Polar bears are excellent swimmers, and they will even stalk seals in the water.

PREY

In addition to coping with the elements, the animals of the Arctic must protect themselves from one of the world's deadliest predators. Here's how two animals try to survive.

HARP SEAL

Harp seals are hide-and-seek masters. They spend much of their time swimming underwater, hunting prey of their own, including fish and shrimp. Every 10 minutes or so, they dare to emerge for a breath of air. When they spend time out of the water, they make holes in the ice for easy access to their hunting grounds.

SCIENTIFIC NAME: *Pagophilus groenlandicus*

TYPICAL LENGTH: 6 feet (1.8 m)

SURVIVAL STRATEGIES

 HIDING

WALRUS

Walruses are too big and too strong to be on the polar bear's regular menu, but they do sometimes find themselves on the losing end of the predator's swat. They have formidable tusks, a 1.5-inch (4-cm) layer of skin, and blubber 6 inches (15 cm) thick.

SCIENTIFIC NAME: *Odobenus rosmarus*

TYPICAL LENGTH: 10 feet (3 m)

SURVIVAL STRATEGIES

 POWER SIZE  TOUGH EXTERIOR WEAPONRY

PUMA

Pumas live all the way from northern Canada to the Southern Andes in South America. They prefer to hunt in areas with dense underbrush, where they can hide, and in rocky outcroppings, from which they can stalk their prey.

Noisy Cats

Even though they can weigh as much as a leopard, pumas are often not counted among the big cats. Like other cats, pumas have a large assortment of vocalizations, including growls, hisses, purrs, yowls, and even an eerie scream.

PUMA

Also known as cougars or mountain lions, these solitary hunters need a lot of room to roam. They usually stalk their prey at dusk and at dawn, silently watching and creeping closer and closer. Finally, they pounce onto the animal's back, breaking its neck with a bite just below the skull. Pumas have powerful legs and can leap up to 20 feet (6 m). If they don't finish eating the kill, they will drag it to a hiding place and bury it. They'll return every night to eat until it's gone.

SCIENTIFIC NAME: *Puma concolor*

TYPICAL LENGTH: 7 feet (2.1 m)

PREY: deer, elk, coyotes, porcupines, badgers, and raccoons

PREDATOR STYLES

POUNCING

POWER

STEALTH

These animals live along the edges of forests and in the grasslands of North America. One relies on numbers for protection, and the other on a good burrow and a sharp set of claws.

ELK

Elk are large members of the deer family. Only the males grow antlers, which can weigh up to 40 pounds (18 kg). However, both males and females can use their powerful hooves to punch at predators. As herd animals, elk are always on the lookout for danger. When distressed, they will bark to warn the others.

SCIENTIFIC NAME: *Cervus elaphus*

TYPICAL LENGTH: 8 feet (2.4 m)

SURVIVAL STRATEGIES

 NUMBERS SIGNALING WEAPONRY

AMERICAN BADGER

A badger will put up a fierce fight if cornered by a predator. If one of its many burrows is nearby, it will back into it snarling, hissing, and baring its teeth. The badger has another advantage. It has a collar of muscle around its neck. Predators have a hard time grabbing on. The badger can also release a stinky smell.

SCIENTIFIC NAME: *Taxidea taxus*

TYPICAL LENGTH: 2.5 feet (.8 m)

SURVIVAL STRATEGIES

 HIDING STINK

RED FOX

Some animals adapt well to living near humans. They take advantage of the open spaces for hunting and foraging.

Beautiful Tail

Also called a brush, a red fox's beautiful, bushy tail helps keep it warm in cold weather. Foxes don't usually dig dens. They lie down with their tails curled around their bodies. Their tails also help them balance when they run.

RED FOX

The red fox is quick and light on its feet. It has an exceptional sense of sight, smell, and hearing, allowing it to easily locate its prey, even underground! Although foxes are related to dogs, they stalk and ambush prey like cats. They hunt alone and at night. Foxes will often stand very still while locating prey. When they find it, they leap straight up in the air and pounce on it with their front paws, pinning the animal to the ground. They also use their paws to dig animals out of their burrows.

SCIENTIFIC NAME: *Vulpes vulpes*

TYPICAL LENGTH: 3.5 feet (1 m)

PREY: rodents, rabbits, and birds

PREDATOR STYLES

AGILITY · HEARING · PATIENCE · POUNCING · SMELLING · STEALTH · VISION

For smaller animals like these, a safe burrow is very important.

EASTERN COTTONTAIL RABBIT

Standing on their hind legs, these rabbits quietly keep watch for predators. But the best defense they have is an amazing ability to jump and change direction almost in midair. When they sense danger, they freeze, and then take off in a fast, zigzag run that is difficult for a predator to follow. (But sometimes they creep away low to the ground instead.) Rabbits have exceptional hearing and will warn other rabbits of a threat with a cry of distress.

SCIENTIFIC NAME: *Sylvilagus floridanus*

TYPICAL LENGTH: 1.5 feet (.5 m)

SURVIVAL STRATEGIES

AGILITY HEARING SIGNALING

SPEED STILLNESS

WHITE-FOOTED MOUSE

These little mice are most concerned with finding or digging a burrow that is safe from predators. They have a habit of drumming their paws on a hollow twig or reed, producing a buzzing noise, which might serve as an alarm call. If a mother mouse senses danger, she will move her babies, one-by-one, to a safer place.

SCIENTIFIC NAME: *Peromyscus leucopus*

TYPICAL LENGTH: 7 inches (18 cm)

SURVIVAL STRATEGIES

HIDING SIGNALING

SERVAL

The serval prowls the waterways, savannas, and forests of central and southern Africa. With their unusually long legs, servals can peek over the tall grasses—and often, their prey doesn't see them.

SERVAL

Servals might be the best hunters of all the cats. Their sandy, spotted coats hide them as they slink through tall grasses and sometimes freeze in place for up to 15 minutes as they listen for prey with their enormous ears. When a serval hears something rustling, its ears turn like radar dishes to find the exact location of the animal. Then, the cat gathers itself and leaps into the air, pouncing on the animal and pinning it down with its front paws. Servals also use this method to catch airborne birds, jumping more than 5 feet (1.5 m) straight up and clapping their paws around them.

SCIENTIFIC NAME: *Leptailurus serval*

TYPICAL LENGTH: 4 feet (1.2 m)

PREY: birds, reptiles, hares, frogs, and insects

PREDATOR STYLES

CAMOUFLAGE HEARING PATIENCE POUNCING

A Highly Successful Hunter

The serval has particularly long, strong legs, which, along with its sensitive hearing, help it hunt efficiently. Unlike most wild cats, servals make a kill in about half of their attempts.

These animals inhabit the marshes and savannas of Africa—prime hunting grounds of the serval. How do they protect themselves?

AFRICAN SPOONBILL

These leggy wading birds have distinctive red legs and faces and spoon-shaped bills. They fish by swinging their bills from side to side to hook fish and insects. Spoonbills are shy and cautious. They are usually solitary birds. When alarmed, they'll let out a loud *Yark-yark!* and take off.

SCIENTIFIC NAME: *Platalea alba*

TYPICAL WINGSPAN: 4 feet (1.2 m)

SURVIVAL STRATEGIES

FLIGHT

SCRUB HARE

This hare has a mottled coat, which helps it blend in with grasses, rocks, and dirt. If a predator comes sniffing around, the scrub hare stays still until the very last moment. Then, it leaps away, zipping right and left to keep the predator off its tail.

SCIENTIFIC NAME: *Lepus saxatilis*

TYPICAL LENGTH: 2 feet (.6 m)

SURVIVAL STRATEGIES

AGILITY CAMOUFLAGE SPEED STILLNESS

SPOTTED HYENA

The animals that live in sub-Saharan Africa inhabit a variety of habitats, from deserts to scrublands to mountains. During the rainy season, many different animals congregate in areas where food and water are plentiful.

The Laughing Hyena

Hyenas are social animals that live in clans of up to 100. They communicate through many different sounds, including their famous cackling "laugh." They usually produce this sound when nervous or when submitting to a dominant female. (Females rule hyena clans.)

SPOTTED HYENA

Although known as scavengers, these intelligent predators get most of their food from live animals they hunt and kill at night. Hyenas use their keen senses of sight, hearing, and smell to detect prey. They work together with their clan members to separate prey from the herd. They can run up to 35 mph (56 kph) for long distances, exhausting their prey before they bring it down. Hyenas eat almost all parts of an animal. Their strong jaws can crush bones and hooves with ease.

SCIENTIFIC NAME: *Crocuta crocuta*

TYPICAL LENGTH: 5 feet (1.5 m)

PREY: wildebeests, zebras, gazelles, Cape buffalo, impalas, and puff adders

PREDATOR STYLES

HEARING   PACK   SMELLING   SPEED   VISION   WEAPONRY

PREY

Many prey animals on the savanna live in herds. Every animal in the herd looks out for danger. Other animals have their own built-in defenses.

IMPALA

Impalas are herd animals, which gives them some safety from predators. When they sense danger, impalas bark a warning, sending the entire herd fleeing. They use their incredible leaping ability to bound away. When running, an impala can cover a distance of 30 feet (9 m) in one leap. They can jump over obstacles up to 10 feet (3 m) high.

SCIENTIFIC NAME: *Aepyceros melampus*

TYPICAL LENGTH: 4.5 feet (1.4 m)

SURVIVAL STRATEGIES

 AGILITY NUMBERS SIGNALING SPEED

PUFF ADDER

Most predators stay away from this cranky reptile. With its long fangs—half an inch (1.3 cm) or longer!—a puff adder can deliver a large amount of extremely poisonous venom to any attacker that dares come too close. A puff adder's coloring provides it with camouflage, but when disturbed, a puff adder will rear up and hiss loudly.

SCIENTIFIC NAME: *Bitis arietans*

TYPICAL LENGTH: 4 feet (1.2 m)

SURVIVAL STRATEGIES

 CAMOUFLAGE VENOM

WESTERN DIAMONDBACK RATTLESNAKE

These predators have a bad reputation throughout southwestern North America. Even horses, deer, and antelope see them as a threat—and may try to stomp on them.

WESTERN DIAMONDBACK RATTLESNAKE

Western diamondback rattlesnakes are known to be excitable and aggressive. They have pits in their faces that detect heat and help them zero in on prey. The snakes, camouflaged by their brownish gray skin, ambush prey animals or seek them out in their burrow, striking quickly and pumping venom into the animals through their tube-shaped fangs. Rattlesnakes often lose their fangs—they break off in the prey animal—but others grow back to take their place. They swallow their prey whole.

SCIENTIFIC NAME: *Crotalus atrox*

TYPICAL LENGTH: 4 feet (1.2 m)

PREY: mice, voles, rabbits, rodents, lizards, and birds

PREDATOR STYLES

The Rattle

The sinister sound of the diamondback's rattle is a warning: *Stay away!* The diamondback adds a new segment to its rattle every time it sheds its skin. Rattlers can shed a couple of times a year.

If you make your home in an open area, such as a prairie, how do you defend yourself? Prairie dogs use a little help from their friends, and the prairie vole has a secret escape.

BLACK-TAILED PRAIRIE DOG

These highly social members of the rodent family live together in large "towns," a series of connected tunnels and burrows with several entrances and exits to help them escape danger. Prairie dogs are always on the lookout for predators. If one is spotted, the alarm whistle goes out—and all in the area immediately drop into the burrow and out of sight.

SCIENTIFIC NAME: *Cynomys ludovicianus*

TYPICAL LENGTH: 1 foot (.3 m)

SURVIVAL STRATEGIES

PRAIRIE VOLE

Slightly larger than field mice, these stout little creatures have an ingenious way to avoid predators. They build tunnels in the soft undergrowth between their burrows and the places where they search for food. If they're out eating and spot a predator, they dart into the tunnel and run back to the safety of the burrow.

SCIENTIFIC NAME: *Microtus ochrogaster*

TYPICAL LENGTH: 6 inches (15 cm)

SURVIVAL STRATEGIES

WOLVERINE

The taiga, or boreal forests, at the far north of the world support a wide range of animal life—from some of the largest carnivores to tiny insects. The cold and lonely forests of the North suit the wolverine, which hunts alone. Male wolverines don't like to share their territory with other males.

WOLVERINE

With their thick, brown fur and padded paws, wolverines look a little like small bears, but they certainly aren't cuddly! Their large paws help them stay on top of the snow, and they can run about 30 mph (48 kph) after prey. They kill their prey with a sharp bite to the neck. Their hooked claws help them climb and catch their prey. Their jaws are powerful enough to crush frozen bones. Wolverines have been known to kill more animals than they can eat. Wolverines have a reputation as fearless, aggressive predators that are unwilling to back down in a fight.

SCIENTIFIC NAME: *Gulo gulo*

TYPICAL LENGTH: 3.5 feet (1 m)

PREY: squirrels, voles, snowshoe hares, birds, deer, and porcupines

PREDATOR STYLES

CLIMBING

POWER

SPEED

Leaving an Odor

Wolverines need large, undisturbed areas in which to live. They mark their territory using scent glands, warning other wolverines to stay away. Sometimes they mark their food caches to keep other animals from eating them.

These prey animals live on different continents, but both prefer northern forests with trees to climb or rocky ledges where they can make quick escapes from possible predators.

SIBERIAN MUSK DEER

These small deer are built differently from other deer, with extremely strong hind legs and weaker, shorter front legs. They are fast and are great leapers. Sometimes they resemble rabbits, because they land with their hind legs in front of their forelegs.

SCIENTIFIC NAME: *Moschus moschiferus*

TYPICAL LENGTH: 3 feet (.9 m)

SURVIVAL STRATEGIES

AGILITY   SPEED

NORTH AMERICAN PORCUPINE

Porcupines use their quills against predators only as a last resort. First, they'll try to get away by climbing a tree. If they can't escape, they'll raise their quills in warning. If the predator isn't deterred, they release a foul-smelling odor. Finally, if the animal comes too close, it will get a snoutful of barbed quills!

SCIENTIFIC NAME: *Erethizon dorsatum*

TYPICAL LENGTH: 3.5 feet (1 m)

SURVIVAL STRATEGIES

CLIMBING   STINK   WEAPONRY

Predator Styles and Prey Survival Strategies

This page sums up the story of predators and prey by laying out the animals' predator styles and survival strategies and by listing the predators and prey that rely on them.

AGILITY
Caracal
Crabeater seal
Dall's porpoise
Easterncottontailrabbit
Fossa
Giant eland
Impala
Kirk's dik-dik
Leopard seal
Mountain goat
Mourning dove
Ocelot
Peregrine falcon
Red fox
Rocky Mountain bighorn
  sheep
Scrub hare
Siberian musk deer
Snowshoe hare
South American fur seal
Verreaux's sifaka
sheep
Verreaux's sifaka
Wolverine

CAMOUFLAGE
Arctic fox
Arctic wolf
Bengal tiger
Cheetah
Giraffe
Golden jackal
Hippopotamus
Hoffmann's two-toed
  sloth
Jaguar
Kirk's dik-dik
Komodo dragon
Leopard
Lion
Mountain goat
Ocelot
Plains zebra
Puff adder
Scrub hare
Serval
Snowshoe hare
Timor deer
Western diamondback
  rattlesnake
Willow ptarmigan

CLIMBING
Chacma baboon
Fossa
Grizzly bear
Hoffmann's two-toed
  sloth
Jaguar
Leopard
Mountain goat
North American
  porcupine
Ocelot
Rocky Mountain bighorn

DECEPTION
Mourning dove
Virginia opossum
Willow ptarmigan

FLIGHT
African spoonbill
Golden eagle
Great horned owl
Lesser flamingo
Peregrine falcon
Willow ptarmigan

HEARING
Arctic fox
Arctic wolf
Caracal
Collared peccary
Easterncottontailrabbit
Gerenuk
Grizzly bear
Leopard
Red fox
Serval
Snowshoe hare
Spotted hyena
Woodchuck

HIDING
American badger
Beaver
Big brown bat
Black-tailed prairie dog
Desert warthog
Harp seal
Hippopotamus
Hoary marmot
Kirk's dik-dik
Nine-banded armadillo
Norway lemming
Prairie vole
Rock hyrax
White-footed mouse
Woodchuck

NUMBERS
Black-tailed prairie dog
Capybara
Caribou
Chacma baboon
Collared peccary
Elk
Emperor penguin
Giant eland
Hoary marmot
Impala
Lesser flamingo
Musk ox
Plains zebra

Rock hyrax
Thomson's gazelle
Timor deer
Water buffalo
Wildebeest

PACK
Arctic wolf
Golden jackal
Gray wolf
Lion
Orca
Spotted hyena

PATIENCE
American alligator
Bengal tiger
Great horned owl
Komodo dragon
Leopard seal
Nile crocodile
Polar bear
Red fox
Serval

POUNCING
Arctic fox
Caracal
Jaguar
Leopard
Ocelot
Puma
Red fox
Serval

POWER
American alligator
Bengal tiger
Caracal
Giraffe
Golden eagle
Great white shark
Green anaconda
Grizzly bear
Jaguar
Komodo dragon
Leopard
Leopard seal
Lion
Musk ox
Nile crocodile
Orca
Plains zebra
Polar bear
Puma
Walrus
Water buffalo
Wolverine

SIGNALING
Beaver
Black-tailed prairie dog
Capybara

Caribou
Chacma baboon
Desert warthog
Easterncottontailrabbit
Elk
Emperor penguin
Gerenuk
Golden jackal
Gray wolf
Hoary marmot
Impala
Muntjac
Norway lemming
Orca
Rock hyrax
Sambar
Thomson's gazelle
Timor deer
Verreaux's sifaka
White-footed mouse
Woodchuck

SIZE
Alligator gar
American alligator
Antarctic minke whale
Bengal tiger
Brazilian tapir
Giraffe
Great white shark
Green anaconda
Grizzly bear
Hippopotamus
Komodo dragon
Loggerhead sea turtle
Moose
Musk ox
Nile crocodile
Orca
Polar bear
Walrus
Water buffalo
Wildebeest

SMELLING
Arctic wolf
Gray wolf
Great white shark
Grizzly bear
Komodo dragon
Red fox
Spotted hyena

SPEED
Alligator gar
Antarctic minke whale
Big brown bat
Capybara
Chacma baboon
Cheetah
Crabeater seal
Dall's porpoise
Easterncottontailrabbit

Emperor penguin
Giant eland
Giraffe
Golden eagle
Gray wolf
Grizzly bear
Impala
Kirk's dik-dik
Leopard
Leopard seal
Moose
Peregrine falcon
Rocky Mountain bighorn
  sheep
Scrub hare
Siberian musk deer
Snowshoe hare
South American fur seal
Spotted hyena
Thomson's gazelle
Wolverine

STEALTH
American alligator
Arctic fox
Bengal tiger
Caracal
Fossa
Great horned owl
Green anaconda
Jaguar
Lion
Nile crocodile
Ocelot
Peregrine falcon
Puma
Red fox

STILLNESS
Desert warthog
Easterncottontailrabbit
Gerenuk
Scrub hare
Snowshoe hare
Willow ptarmigan

STINK
American badger
North American
  porcupine
Southern tamandua
Striped skunk

SWIMMING
Beaver
Brazilian tapir
Capybara
Green anaconda
Hoffmann's two-toed
  sloth
Jaguar
Komodo dragon
Leopard

Moose
Nile crocodile
Ocelot
Polar bear
Sambar

TOUGH EXTERIOR
Loggerhead sea turtle
Nine-banded armadillo
Walrus

VENOM
Komodo dragon
Puff adder
Western diamondback
  rattlesnake

VISION
Fossa
Golden eagle
Great horned owl
Jaguar
Leopard
Ocelot
Peregrine falcon
Red fox
Rocky Mountain bighorn
  sheep
Spotted hyena

WEAPONRY
Caribou
Chacma baboon
Collared peccary
Desert warthog
Elk
Giant eland
Giraffe
Golden eagle
Great white shark
Highland streaked tenrec
Hippopotamus
Hoffmann's two-toed
  sloth
Moose
Mountain goat
Muntjac
Musk ox
Nile crocodile
North American
  porcupine
Rocky Mountain bighorn
  sheep
Sambar
Southern tamandua
Spotted hyena
Timor deer
Walrus
Water buffalo
Wildebeest
Woodchuck

Red = predators
Green = prey